*"our words*
*like bolts of lightning in a dark night*
*lighting our way*
*our words*
*like tears like rain like cries like hail from our hearts*
*feeling with each other in our suffering for each other"*

— Bud Osborn (1947-2014)


*"Poetry is what happens when nothing else can."*

— Charles Bukowski (1920-1994)

# POEMS

## HENRY DOYLE

ANVIL PRESS • VANCOUVER

LIBRARY AND ARCHIVES CANADA CATALOGUING IN PUBLICATION

Title: No shelter : poems / Henry Doyle.
Names: Doyle, Henry, author.
Identifiers: Canadiana 20210263431 | ISBN 9781772141832 (softcover)
Classification: LCC PS8607.O98853 N6 2021 | DDC C811/.6—dc23

Edited for the press by Fiona Tinwei Lam
Cover and interior images by Richard Tetrault
Cover design by Derek von Essen
Interior layout and design by HeimatHouse

Represented in Canada by Publishers Group Canada
Distributed by Raincoast Books

The publisher gratefully acknowledges the financial assistance of the Canada Council for the Arts, the Canada Book Fund, and the Province of British Columbia through the B.C. Arts Council and the Book Publishing Tax Credit.

Anvil Press Publishers Inc.
P.O. Box 3008, Main Post Office
Vancouver, B.C. V6B 3X5 CANADA
www.anvilpress.com

PRINTED AND BOUND IN CANADA

*Dedicated to my poetry mentors,*
*Fiona Tinwei Lam*
*and*
*Elee Kraljii Gardiner*

# Table of Contents

## I.

## II.

## III.

## IV.

**I.**

# The White Horse

I'm six years old in my third foster home,
always hiding in my top floor room,
gazing out the window onto the ocean
of wheat, the fields rippling like waves,
tractors rolling over the land like great ships.

After another beating, I raid the fridge,
filling a brown paper bag,
making sure I have carrots.
I run out of the house, away
from the farmhouse and barns
to a fenced-off plot of land
which holds that single white horse
I've been watching since I arrived.
He waits for me, heaven-sent.
I open the gate, give him a carrot.
His big nostrils blow steam in my face.
I laugh for the first time in a year.
I give him another, climb the fence,
then onto his back, wishing
to ride him to freedom.
But I fall, landing underneath his belly.
He steps back carefully, one hoof at a time.
Winded, I look up at him
as he gazes down at me
with sky-blue northern eyes,
his muzzle nuzzling my face,
making sure I'm okay.
My hand comes up with another carrot.

My great escape is a bust,
but I make a friend that day.

# The House on Cooper Street

So many hours riding by train, bus and car
to just another foster home.
This time, six kids
in a three storey house full of rats.

The Sealtest Dairy factory is across the street.
At 5 AM the sound of air brakes
from milk trucks turning the corner
always wakes me up.

I love my little room at the back:
a gray cot, a dresser
and an escape route.

I climb out my window
onto the back door overhang, then drop down
to raid the factory dumpsters
for the returned milk jugs
with the little holes in them,
cash them in again at corner stores,
buy comic books, chocolate milk, chips,
and candy bars, but
Hot Wheels cars are my favourite.

Each weekend, I join the neighbourhood kids
behind the Ottawa Boys' Club,
laying down plastic tracks on the hill.
Everyone's racing,
hoping to win.

# The Hippies

A beating after supper puts me on the run.
Nine years old. No coat, just a T-shirt.
I run through the September downpour,
heading for the National Arts Centre
at the back of the canal. I stop, wide-eyed.
A dozen or more hippies
are camped out under the overhang.
Dressed in army fatigues and tie-dyed shirts,
they rise from their sleeping bags.
Picking up a blanket, a woman inches forward.
Long blond hair, big green eyes,
a colourful skirt hanging down to her bare feet.
She stretches out her hand, trying to coax me over.
Like a trapped animal with nowhere to go,
I take a step forward.
She wraps a thick warm blanket around me.
Other women come over.
One dries off my hair with a towel.
A guy with long hair and a beard
gives me an open can of beans,
sits beside me, starts playing guitar.
"Wish you were my parents," I say.
The woman who gave me the blanket
sits beside me all night long.

The next morning, I walk with them
to the bus station. Half of them leave
for New York, the other half for Toronto.
I wave goodbye, then head to the highway
to hitchhike and follow them.
But the police nab me before I can.

# Dead Time, Innis Road

I walk into Max Three, a punk kid who's just turned seventeen
serving eight months dead time before sentencing.

The guards take me down the cell range with my bedroll
to 13-B at the end of the 26-cell unit
through wolf calls from real bank robbers,
prisoners from the 1950s and 60s with short greaser haircuts.

The old prisoners have lived there a long time —
the only thing they've done right. None of them
bother me, but nickname me "Mary"
because my long hair hangs down to my elbows.

The young guys keep fighting me
and I get thrown in the hole, in and out
so many times, the guards call me Yo-Yo Boy.
In that small brick room, I am alone and safe,
a Bible for a pillow on the steel frame bed.

# Maplehurst

18 hours of blinding light.
11 PM — beautiful darkness.
A mattress. Nightmares.
5 AM — the lights come on.
The heavy metal door opens.
Guards who fought in the Korean War
rush in, barking their orders,
drag you to the floor,
yank out the mattress.
"Stop using your Bible for a fuck'n pillow
or we will take it away."

Under the heavy smock
made of moving blankets,
you're naked.
"Stand up, convict.
Bend over, spread your cheeks."
All three guards take a good look.
One of them says,
"Good, he hasn't been raped yet."

The walls of the 6 by 6 foot cell
are painted puke green.
A steel bed frame, stainless steel toilet, sink.
Beancake for breakfast, lunch, dinner:
mashed potatoes and beans in between
two pieces of white bread.
A cup of tea. You pick out
the snot on the bread, pour out the tea
that a guard has spit in.

On the fourteenth day of solitary,
you get a regular meal. One guard says,
"We're making sure
you never come back."

# Gladiator

In society, I am terrified.
No confidence, no hope.
But when I step into that squared circle,
I have no fear.

Climbing those metal stairs,
pulling the ropes, I'm a gladiator.
Crowds cheer and boo me.
Through blood and sweat,
I wear an invisible smile.

At 139 pounds, I'm a dirty, hate-filled fighter
after doing two years in jail
with a year's dead-time, beaten
by men twice my size,
my soul's rage searching
for honour.

After hundreds of fights
in Hull, Ottawa, Buffalo, and Montreal,
I become my own country,
my own king.

## Beautiful Loser

A long bus ride from Montreal back to Ottawa,
body and spirit in a fog.
We stop at a highway restaurant.
Everyone is talking about that last fight.
My fight.

How I got knocked down
by a guy 10 pounds heavier than me,
twice in the first round,
twice in the second,
twice in the third.
Grabbed those ropes,
pulled myself up into more
and more punishment,
the crowd going crazy.

I sit in a far corner booth.
two black eyes, bloodied tissue up my nose.
My trainer comes up to me.
"How are you doing, kid?"

"This is the fourth in a row.
I feel like a loser, coach."
"Kid," he grabs my shoulder,
"You might've lost that fight tonight,
but you were beautiful."

## Raging Bull, 1982

Just back in Ottawa with two fresh black eyes
from losing a match in Montreal,
I stand in line with my girlfriend Leanne
at the movie theatre down on Elgin street.
We get seats and popcorn,
but we don't eat a single kernel
because she starts getting angry.
"You are just like this asshole!
You swear just like him!"
Maybe she's right.
I do swear a lot.
I try to kiss her, feel her up a bit,
but through the whole movie
she'll have nothing to do with me.
I don't stop swearing or boxing,
but I get another girlfriend.

## Remembrance Day

At the last fight I lose
at the Golden Gloves in Hull,
my father shows up, the first time
I've seen him since I was eight.
He takes me out for a steak dinner.
"Warriors eat meat," he says with a proud smile
as I sit, aching, with blackened eyes.
"Steak was the first meal I ate
coming back from the war.
I wasn't much older than you are now."
He'd trained with thirty-nine soldiers in Scotland.
Shimmied to the front of their boat on D-Day
to be the first off in Normandy.
Each of those thirty-nine died.

I didn't really know him.
When my mother disappeared,
he put me into foster care.
He married a tall, beautiful German woman.
She told me that after the war
when the German tanks returned to her city,
she and her teenage friends would jump on them.
"But the tanks were so hot from American gunfire,
we'd all jump off just as fast!"

At twenty-four, I quit boxing to try to join the army.
Behind the desk, the needle-nosed officer
his chest covered with medals, reads my mind:
"I'm not going to train an ex-con like you for five years
so you can become a mercenary."

When my dad has a heart attack,
I visit him in the hospital.
His roommate is an old German soldier
who doesn't speak English.
As his wife translates for the nurses,
my father glares across the room.
His look says "You bastards."

After my father's death,
I start my own tradition: every year,
I take off my poppy, pour out a beer
by the cenotaph, then drink a toast
to the old man and those fallen thirty-nine.

**II.**

# Down & Out in Ottawa

Ottawa is my bad luck city.
Haven't been back in ten years. No wonder
the clutch blew out on my Triumph.
The Sally Ann lets me park it
at the back of the building.
I stay for eighteen months
in the basement dormitory
while my bike gets rebuilt.
A ripple in my life.

$6 a night for a bed, $42 a week,
meals not included.
Church mandatory on Sundays.
twenty cots with gray army-style bedding.
Beside them, metal chairs with tin can ashtrays.
Every couple of feet, a sign on the wall:

> **ATTENTION**
> If you smoke in bed, make sure
> you have one foot on the floor at all times.

On worn wooden pews, old wino war vets
with their potato faces, mushroom noses,
and Aqua Velva breath
keep me company. Time
hangs off their melting skin
as they doze. I'm wide awake,
my nerves digging their way out of me.

I leave after the morning service,
my unwashed hair hanging down past my shoulders,
tattered blue jeans tucked inside cowboy boots,

holes in the soles stuffed with cardboard,
heels worn down to wood and nails
grinding on the sidewalk.

I wander around lost
in my own hometown.

# Junkyard

### i. Labour Pool, Ottawa

I walk into an old house
that's become a labour pool office.
The plank floors creak with age,
the living room now a waiting room
with over twenty men. In a corner,
there's a card table where they're playing
a jailhouse game of Biz Whist.
Most are ex-cons like me who can't get a real job.
But this is the only place to push back
from being pushed down.

"What's the job here that nobody wants?" I ask.
Everyone replies at once, "The junkyard!"
There's a loudmouth in every pack.
He sits there, short and chunky, with a dented nose,
thick black hair and beard.
"Don't work on the docks, man.
Try to work in the yard."
The others nod.

I go to the office in the kitchen.
"Do you need a worker for the junkyard?"
The only way to claw my way out
of a deep well.

## ii. Old Stanley and the Bibles

I ride with a half dozen men seated on milk crates
in the back of a beat-up white van.
The industrial road is packed
with transport trucks stacked
with flattened cars from Montreal and Detroit.

From the front gate, we see trucks
go over to the weigh house before dumping their loads.
The yard is a forest of steel. Row upon row
of stacked crushed cars, twenty or more high.
A huge crane on top of a hill roars like a monster,
its sixty-foot claw arm lifting cars
through heavy black smoke.
On the other side of the yard
is a jagged twenty-foot heap
of rusted beams and big hunks of metal
too big for the shredder, waiting
to get sliced up for shipping.

My new boss is Old Stanley, a tall man
with crew cut silver hair and denim overalls.
Shaking my hand, he proudly tells me,
"This is the third largest junkyard in North America."

Inside the noisy concrete engine room,
the air smells of grease and steel.
Submarine engines from 1942 and 1945
as big as houses turn two carbines
with three-hundred-pound hammers to shred
whole cars into inches of metal.

He shows me a row of a dozen lockers,
with mine labelled "Yardsman Checker"

beside a bookcase with eight shelves full of bibles.
On the bottom, paperback versions.
Leather ones higher up. I reach
for the top shelf. The biggest Bible —
a foot wide, a foot and a half long, six inches thick,
covered in old horsehide leather.
I feel its weight in my hands,
then brush off years of reddish dust.

Touching the cover's gold lettering,
something expands in my chest
on that cold January day. I open
the book, turn gilt-edged pages,
then notice the date: 1887.

On other shelves, other holy books —
the Torah, Koran, Russian Bibles
all covered in rust dust.

With smiling eyes, Old Stanley tells me,
"If you find a bible of any kind, put it here
to keep it safe and out of the shredder.
It's bad luck for the yard."

I start my job removing tires and gas tanks.
That first week, I pull a tank out through the back door
of this big brown station wagon
with a smashed-up front end.
I find my first one: a Gideon Bible,
probably from some US hotel.

I run up the hill, knowing
I've just saved something important.
The shredder won't be shut down by God now.

### iii. Odin

At 7 AM, I get off the bus.
Outside the scrap metal yard, a mile-long line
of flatbed trucks. Inside the fence,
a line of over twenty cats. One cat in front
with thick, long black fur, striped with white
from the top of his huge head to his back,
and only one eye. I name him
Odin, after the God of Valhalla
who gave up an eye for knowledge.
The night guard opens the gate.
"They're waiting for you, kid."

Every day I walk through the yard
while all the cats follow me,
kittens clawing up the side of my jeans, eager
for breakfast. By the time I get to the office,
I'm covered in kittens.

Putting away their gear one day,
the night crew laughs.
"Maybe we should build these cats a doghouse."
By the end of the week, they build
the biggest doghouse I've ever seen.
Painted orange, four by three feet,
a tin roof over a wooden frame,
different sized entry holes cut into the sides,
interior insulated with carpet patches.

At 4 PM the shredder shuts down.
The sound of grinding stops.
Cats emerge from nowhere,
taking over the yard, following me with their meows.

Just like Old Stanley showed me,
I grab the fifty-pound bag of cat food from storage,
then haul it to the dog house.
Kittens are fed first with small bowls of food and milk.
A huge steel bowl filled for the others.

Odin is a killer: any threats to his reign
found dead in the morning.
He answers to his name, but never lets me touch him.
Just watches me from three feet away
while I talk, throwing him treats.

Years later, I'll still remember
how he'd come to the fence to say goodbye
every night, watching me leave
with his one green eye glowing.

## iv.  Steel Mountain

For two years, I keep that monster shredder fed
from 7 AM to 4 PM
so it never needs to shut down.

Dump trucks arrive, full
of old dishwashers, washers and dryers,
cigarette vending machines, car parts.
I climb up behind the trucks to sort out
the metals that can go through the shredder
without jamming it up, picking out heavy pieces
for the other pile across the yard.

Little John, a short French Canadian in his sixties,
runs the forklift, bringing flattened cars to Ron,
the hard-ass crane operator at the top of the hill,
who feeds them head first into the shredder.

The 940 CAT front-end loader
keeps filling up its bucket and driving up
the mountain of steel to dump its load.
The mountain grows to over ten storeys,
the highest it's ever been.
Smoke covers the junkyard like black fog.

A red plywood shack is my office.
I sit on a bar stool beside a folding table,
a propane heater underneath.
On cold days, I run inside to warm up,
then run back out when trucks arrive.
In and out all day, counting the cars,
filling out forms for the weigh house.
A couple times a month, I'll dive for cover

when gas tanks left behind in cars explode
in the shredder like grenades, shrapnel flying,
hitting my shack's tin roof.

On November 11, the bosses arrive,
four tall Jewish brothers in sunglasses.
Their $1000 suits glitter in the sun.
I feel like a border guard
from some developing nation.
Behind me is destruction.

Stretching out their hands to shake mine,
they tell me that today I have broken
the junkyard's tonnage record for steel production
from WWII and the Korean War.
*The world isn't at war anymore,*
*but I guess I am*, I think.

They give me a $500 bonus cheque,
but after the labour pool accountant takes its cut,
I get $375. And they still don't offer me
a full-time job.

## v. The Accident

A few weeks before Christmas,
a double-loaded dump truck arrives off the weigh scale
with three huge industrial air conditioners
on top of heaps of steel wire.
Getting a cut for every pound of copper and aluminum,
I feel like a gold miner.

I heave one air conditioner onto the loader.
Little John drives it to the weigh house while I turn back,
up to my waist in wire,
trying to free the other air conditioner.
But the massive blade of the loader
rams into my back. I scream
and fall, legs entangled in wire beneath the blade.

Little John can't hear over the shredder.
He can't see with the sun in his eyes.
His radio's off. I'm screwed.

I get dragged over gravel
toward the concrete pad where I know
the lowered blade will crush my legs.
Strangely calm, I shimmy down
so it lies on my chest to kill me fast.

A foot away from the pad,
the blade stops, rises, backs away.

I stand up, dust myself off.
Ron, the crane operator, tells me he saw it all.
He'd thrown chunks of steel at Little John's cab
to get his attention.

I'm driven to the hospital, released hours later.
I'm scraped down my back, legs bruised,
but don't feel the pain until next morning.
After a few days, I return to the yard.
My new nickname, "Dead Man Walking."
Ron says, "You owe me a beer for saving your miserable life."
I look around. Everyone's now wearing orange safety vests.
They've replaced me with a young moron
who's already shut down the shredder three times.

It's over. I can't go back
to the hardest, best job I'll ever have.

# 1991

A full moon in front of me,
I ride out of Ottawa
in the cold night air
like an outcast wolf.

My 650 chopper howls down the 401
at eighty-eight miles per hour.
Heading back to Toronto.
Another skid row.
Another hotel room.
Another labour pool job.

I fight with my machine
so I don't get dragged under
all those 18-wheelers
passing like freight trains,
one after the other,
like a 120 mile per hour hurricane.

Free, alive,
the devil on my back.

## Ghost in the Closet

I move into this rooming house.
There's an opening because some poor dude
hanged himself in the closet.

The landlord nails the closet door shut
with six nails. He tells me
he's taking $10 off my rent
because of the closet space.
Great, more beer money.

"You're not scared of ghosts, are you, Joe?"
"Why should I be, the closet door is nailed shut."

I get a 12-pack from the beer store,
then buy a hammer at the hardware store.
Go back to my room and take out all
the nails from my closet.
Just in case the ghost wants out.

# No Room Left for Angels

Working night shift
in a food factory warehouse
at the end of the subway line in Scarborough.

It's 4 AM in a bad dream,
working those jobs that
losers take.

Legs feel like hollow lead pipes.
My soul empties
in dark corners.

Thinking of this chick, I take a break,
jerk off first, then light a smoke.
Look into the mirror.

Hidden in its grey fog, haunted red eyes
stare back, fearing
there is no room left
for angels anymore.

## All-Day Breakfast

"Meet my new girlfriend," he says with a big red-moustached smile.

She had that street-wise sex appeal about her, long painted eyes and thick red lips that I didn't trust, but guys like us with our lives on fire never got laid much.

I didn't even smile. I could see that she was only digging him until his wallet dried up.

We slept at all-night skid row coffee shops when there weren't any beds at the Sally-Ann or went down to the rathole Korean theatre on Yonge Street, paying $5 a night to stay the weekend, drinking cheap vodka and selling black hash. The staff would walk up and down the aisles with bamboo poles, nudging us awake at 5 AM on Sundays. When the theatre lights would come on, it was like a coffin had opened. I would walk out into Yonge Street's emptiness.

The first thing I did was count the money I made selling hash, then head for Sophie's down on Parliament at Queen. We'd all lurk in the back like stray dogs from society, drinking beer in big coffee mugs. When we did have girlfriends, we thought we'd struck gold. But it always turned out to be fool's gold.

It was welfare week, the best time to go into the labour pools because everyone was on a drunk or paying rent. It was after 4 PM, and I'd just cashed in three or four days of work slips. I was heading for the Canada House Tavern down on Queen and Sherbourne Street to have a few beers and pick up an ounce of black hash and start all over again.

"We are going to that all-day breakfast thing they have now. Do you want to come along, Joe?" Scotty asked.

Serving bacon and eggs after 4 PM will never catch on, I thought.

"No thanks, man," I said, and wished them well and headed for the tavern. It's funny when you don't see a buddy from the streets for a while. You figure that they are in jail or in love.

Both are hell in the end.

## Shotguns in the Sky

> "The rotting of a heart..."
>     — Charles Bukowski, from "Practice"
>     in *The Roominghouse Madrigals*

The bus from Montreal is late.

I turn my pockets inside out in the rain,
dreaming of shotguns in the sky.

My rotting heart sings in the downpour.
Alice's big white rabbit comes by

and gives me a gram of magic mushrooms
to rescue me from your world.

## The Last Bus

It's the last bus of the night.
We night-shift workers from the steel factory
down on the Lakeshore get on.
Heavy boots marching,
covered in metal dust.
I find an empty seat,
comfortable darkness.
The rain falls on the windows
like shooting spider webs.
Car headlights pass like flashes
of past lives. My biggest worry
is to make it
to the bar for last call.

**III.**

## Slave Labour Pool

I'm 44 with my last unemployment cheque
and nothing to lose.
I buy a one-way plane ticket from Toronto to Vancouver.
I arrive, then take a bus to the train station
with an old suitcase full of socks, underwear, a pair of work jeans,
Bukowski's poetry and a manual typewriter.
I walk out of the station and stand
in the park across the road.

It's the fourth of July, my birthday.
I stare at the mountains to the north, then look south
to see my first SkyTrain pulling into its stop above
on columns resembling Roman aqueducts.
I feel like I'm in the future,
no longer in Toronto.
Head for the station to check it out,
wanting a coffee. Crossing Terminal and Main,
I notice a familiar sight —

a crowd of men in steel-toed boots
smoking cigarettes and drinking coffee.
The building resembles a World War II bunker
with its huge cement slabs at a 45-degree angle
and a single entrance.

I walk in down a ramp into a large green room.
Hardened men melt into the long rows of chairs,
working men like me.
Tasting the cement dust in the air,
I feel at home again.

The first time I ever walked into a labour pool,
I'd just turned 17, coming back
from picking tobacco in Southern Ontario
with $900 in my pocket.
I never returned to high school.

At the front of the room, a young man dressed in black
with blue suspenders and chopped black hair
calls out names and hands out work slips
behind a long, high desk.
Seeing a stack of applications,
I take one with a clipboard.
Sit down in the back to fill it out,
a heap of mountain bikes behind me.

I hand in my application, feel like a beggar
asking for more soup, looking up at this
well-dressed man sitting heavy on his throne.
Taking a quick look at it, he says,
"Be here tomorrow at 6 AM
and I will put you back to work."

I leave the bunker and head for skid row,
looking for a room. I walk down East Hastings,
pass by alleys stinking of urine.
Gray ghosts in hoodies run back and forth like rats.
A gauntlet of drug addicts and dealers.
"Rock, powder, down, rock, powder, down, rock, powder, down."

By the bottle depot, a line of people with shopping carts
waiting for the warehouse to open.
The harsh dead smell of stale beer overwhelms me.
I find a tree and puke.
The whole block, a scene out of a Mad Max movie.

The place packed tight with hundreds
of street people sleeping in cardboard tents.
Their shopping carts, their home.
In a closed down storefront, a dude shoots up
another guy in the neck. Chemical clouds
of crack cocaine and weed in the air.

Blankets spread out on the sidewalks with everything
from canned food to electronics. A junkie flea market.
Harm Reduction garbage everywhere:
syringes, cookers, blue tabs of water, rubber ties.

Next day, I trade in my cowboy boots
for rubber steel-toed construction boots.
After work, I go to the Ivanhoe.
"Buy two beer and we cash your cheque. Just sign here,"
says the bartender, his long-lined highway face set in stone.
I get my two mugs of beer and head for the smoking room,
dead end dreams haunting me,
trying to drag me down.
But I hold on, knowing
that I'm still here and free.
I'm still paying my own way.
I'm still a working man.

# Refugees from Nowhere

I stand in a long line, waiting
for the city shelter's doors to open
down on Cordova Street.

A cop van pulls up
and they start handing out
new sleeping bags
like we are refugees
from nowhere.

We're each given a mat on the gym floor,
a pillow and a grey blanket.
I ask for a wake-up call for 5 AM.

My brand new construction boots tied together
and hung around my neck,
I come back from the toilet
in the middle of the night,
step into the low-lit stink and notice

we all look like plane crash victims
in zipper bags.

## Poetry of a Square Room

Battered brown door.
8 by 10 foot room.
Bed against far corner
covered by grayish sheet.
Old round bar table with ashtray.
Yellow, smoke-stained walls.
Window onto brick.
Small sink with cracked mirror.
Radio playing "Stairway to Heaven".
Welfare Wednesday
running down the hallway.

I lock the door.
Sit down at the table.
One run-down hotel room in Toronto traded
for another on the west coast.
Graffiti on the wall
in thick black ink:

> *Death Is Alive Here*
> *Hate Is Real Here*
> *God Doesn't Exist Here*
> *Welcome to the DTES*

## Death Isn't Lonely

A crow sits in a skeleton winter tree above
a homeless man covered by a yellow sheet.
His empty wheelchair, his tombstone.

# Rooming House Blues

I sit here by my TV,
turn away from a pizza commercial,
peel myself out of my dumpster-bin La-Z-Boy.
Look into my cupboard.
Only Kraft Dinner, stale brown bread
and peanut butter —
a Food Bank, skid row survival kit.
I head out in the winter rain for the soup kitchen
that gives free meals with religion.
I stand there hungry,
a piece of cardboard for an umbrella.
Take a seat beside some dude
who looks twenty years older than he really is
and smells like an open Listerine bottle.
On the other side is a little old man
curled up in his chair as if it were a bed,
stinking of urine.
He shivers the cold streets off his body,
looking around with saucer eyes
as if bombs are going off.
Then, a twenty-five-minute sermon
for a three-minute meal.
I stand up against the back wall,
wishing for a blindfold and that last cigarette.
We're packed in here like starving cattle
on the way to Vonnegut's slaughterhouse.

# Killing Me the Rest of the Way

*For Al Purdy*

The bar is closing,
the doors locked.
The bartender is cashing out.
The waitress with big pancake breasts is counting tips.
The barroom cleaner puts chairs on tables.
The end of another slave labour pool work week.
I sit finishing off a mug of beer,
empty mugs in front of me.
I stare into the mirror behind the bar:
Long, tangled, cement-dust hair,
hardened, tortured hands,
hard hat,
work gloves,
tool belt,
hammer,
nails scattered out onto the bar.
It's been a week of digging holes,
jackhammering four storeys underground.
I look across the deserted bar.
"Drink up Joe, Hell is closed,"
the bartender laughs
out the side of his mouth.
Killing me the rest of the way.

# Pain & Wastings

A city tour bus stops at the corner of Main and Hastings,
full of wide-eyed tourists gawking
at women who look like witches from Polanski's *Macbeth*,
and men, like starving vampires
circling the DTES drain.

Their drugs bring them to heaven,
but they wake up on cardboard beds.
They sleep, shit, piss and fuck
in back alleys through
that vicious sting of urine.

Angry shrieks wake me up at 4 AM.
Three women fight off a drunk.
Looking out the Shaldon Hotel window,
I curse them and pray for them in one breath.

I walk through the junkie flea market.
Stop at one spot with a thin-faced girl
with jade green eyes.
She crouches over her stuff
like an alley cat over rats.

A horde live under the United We Can canopy.
Society's shipwreck survivors.
Hunters with garbage bin traplines,
their shopping carts full of cans and bottles
singing down broken sidewalks.

As they light up their crack pipes,
little pieces of their souls
burn into the night.

# Hey Joe

He sees her at the corner every morning
just before 6 AM,
both of them survivors.
She wears that painted professional smile.
He's wearing worn-out construction boots.
She walks up to him, swaying on invisible waves,
long bare legs in laced black boots.
"Hey Joe, you got a smoke? How's your war going?"
"Losing with a smile on," he says.
 "Why's life so hard on you?"
"Because God's a bigger drunk than I am."
She laughs, grasps his arm.
"Do you have any dreams?"
"Yeah, two mugs of beer at the end of my workday."
A car pulls up. She says,
"No rest for the wicked."

One morning, she's there at the bar,
her legs folded together like a flower.
Her long fingers ripple hello.
They're the only ones there.
She sits with her double vodka, he with his beer.
"How's your war going today?"
she says with her full-lipped smile.
"Me and God don't fight on Sundays.
We just get drunk together."
She laughs like a songbird.
"You have an old soul, Joe.
Come home with me."

Until the sun surrenders to darkness,
he'll climb up and down her long body.
Kiss every part of her, eyes wide open.

# Underground Room

Drinking away yesterday,
I look into today's black hole.
Type out a lost life.

I head out to the slave labour pool.
I put my mark on the worksheet.
The place is as packed as a can of rotten sardines.
An old man sleeping in his work boots
has pissed himself. Moving seats,
I watch the scrawny drug addicts
get all the jobs.

I end up on a construction site
making $8 an hour working
beside some kid half my age.
Contempt in his eyes, he tells me
he's making $22.50 an hour.
Society has tried to stop me
from becoming a loser, but destiny
hangs its heavy sign upon me.

Standing on the bus,
tool belt over a sore shoulder.
Would sell my soul for a seat.
Feels like I'm on a U-Boat.
Bully my way through
to get off at Main Street,
not polite, not Canadian.
I march through rush hour
to pick up a cheque — $64 minus
the $12 government fee.

At the Ivanhoe, gripping my mugs of beer,
I head for the smoking room,
sit in the corner,
drop my tool belt on the floor,
land in the nearest chair like a crashing plane.
Down the first mug in silence and pain.
Take out pen and paper to write out
all my madness before returning
underground.

## Broken Key

A miztake from zkid-row
that drinkz too much
zmokez too much
and thinkz too much

A miztake that'z been "On the Road" too long
fightz hiz demonz with a zmile on
and zpitz in the eye of God

A miztake that knowz hiz way to Hell
and will never leave thiz room
A mistake that'z lozt in hiz typewriter
Juzt a miztake
that can never be erazed

# Drunken Laundry Day with Charles Bukowski

It takes a six-pack just for him to get it together
in that dirty underground room of his.
His radio is cranked, "London Calling."
He gets his mess together into a pile.
Condemned rags, he thinks,
and cracks another beer.

With a pillowcase and a box of soap,
he heads out with that beer-stained
book of Bukowski poems,
*The Days Run Away Like Wild Horses Over the Hills*
to the laundromat around the corner.
The cashier is on his left.
The rat-tat-tat of a sewing machine
behind the counter. He goes to the back.
Chairs, tables, scattered newspapers.
He stuffs his stinky rags into a washer.
He stays and reads Bukowski,
puts his workman's rags into the dryer,
sinks enough quarters in for an hour,
and heads for that closest bar.

"I'll have two of your cheapest draft,"
he says to the young bartender.
He puts the book down
to get at a twenty-dollar bill.
"I think Mr. Bukowski would approve,"
the bartender says. "I read his shit in college.
A lot of us have, dude."
He heads for that sooty fishbowl smoking room,
thinks, all right, college students
still read Bukowski.

After the third round and another poem,
"Song of my typewriter,"
he goes back out in sunglasses
through a gauntlet of drug addicts
curled up in grubby blankets.
Syringes scattered with garbage everywhere.
Skinny, hardened, rat-faced drug addicts
committing suicide slowly.
This twenty-year-old kid jumps
in front of him, wrapped in a blanket,
holding a garbage bag suitcase, asking
"Do you want to buy some crack?"
Thin, tall, shaggy blond hair, blue eyes,
a sculpted bronze sunken pimpled face,
bare, grimy feet — like a fallen angel.
"No, my life is hard enough kid,
I don't have to make it any harder, man."

He stumbles into the laundromat,
feeling like he just escaped a bunch of zombies.
The place is full of the extinct middle class.
He watches them as they slowly turn into fossils,
feels more pity for them
than the ones that are outside
committing suicide.

He opens the dryer door.
"Jesus Christ, hot as hell!" he says out loud.
Bangs his head, curses in silence.
Then he hears a little voice.
"Mommy, there's another man arguing with God again."
He turns around, takes off his sunglasses.
A little girl with sun-kissed freckles smiles.
As she sits there on the table,

her mother continues folding their clothes.
With a smile she says, "Let the man be, Sara."
"My laundry is really hot," he says,
in his own mad defence.

He stuffs his rags into his pillowcase,
thinks only of that other warm six-pack.
Says goodbye to the little girl and her mother.
Apologizes to them and God.
Returns underground to drink and read
Bukowski's drunken knowledge.

# The DTES Alarm Clock

*For Dave Dickson*

*"Quothe the Raven, 'Nevermore.'"*
    – Edgar Allan Poe

If the drug-crazed screams don't wake me up at 4 AM,
city fire trucks and ambulances screaming
around the corner of Main and Hastings will.
Cop cars circle skid row hotels
while addicts and dealers scatter.
I crawl out of bed to get my hangover a beer.
Put a blank piece of paper into my old typewriter
to escape from life down here. It's pushing 5 AM.
Like wild elephants, the city's front-end loaders
attack back alley dumpsters, steel on steel.
Transit buses wail up and down the street.
The DTES alarm clock is about to go off.
Under streetlamps, shadowy crows spread their wings
like thunderbirds in the darkness.

# The Untouchables

*For Ashley Machiskinic*

The cops have captured another drug addict mule.
Her skinny body shivers in the high afternoon sun,
the handcuffs on her wrists melting off.
On the hood of the cop car, the contents
of her black lace purse are scattered out —
crack pipe, syringes and a fresh baggie of rock cocaine.
Like a wild animal in a hunter's trap, she shivers for her ragged life.
Not because she is going to jail. She'll be released
in the morning with a court date. She shivers,
looking across the street at the untouchable
drug dealers who gave her the drugs.
They look back at her like hungry wolves.
They'll beat her, strip her naked,
throw her backwards out the window,
her running shoes tossed out twenty seconds later.

## Ten Years Later

I'm not too old for this,
I say to myself.
They get younger every time,
talking about girls in high school —
ones that were loose, ones that weren't.

It's the usual gig: construction cleanup.
Heavy bristle broom, shovel and garbage can,
sweeping, picking up drywall and pieces of wood,
moving from one condo to another.

At construction sites, I was always at the bottom,
but I feel it stronger today. Every time
it's that one guy who makes three times what I do
that bums a smoke. I hand it over,
feeling like I have a gun to my head.
I don't wait for the thanks, walk away fast
to bury myself in work.

Their young faces gaze at me with pity.

*I'm not too old for this.*
*I'm not too old for this.*
*I'm not too old for this.*

**IV.**

# Aftermath

At 4:30 AM
a big rig-ladder firetruck
thunderclaps around my corner,
violently shaking me awake.

I puke while brushing my teeth.
Haven't showered in days.
I put on hard-crusted socks,
underwear, black T-shirt,
Dickies work pants — the kind
with all those great pockets —
and ugly steel-toed boots.

In the kitchen, there are three open warm beers
and four T3s. I chew them
thinking of blackboard chalk,
washing them down with the beer.

I march to a four-storey, one-hundred-year-old
SRO building with no elevator.
Lives jammed into a hundred
6 by 8 foot rooms.

No one ever calls me by name,
just "Boss." The dozen keys
and brick-sized two-way radio
hanging off my work belt remind them
of doing time. They tell me,
"You get to go home from this place,
but we're stuck here."

I do a building check:

24 toilets, 12 showers, 18 extra-large garbage cans.
A soldier surveying a battlefield
on the aftermath of Welfare Wednesday.

Blood-spattered bathrooms walls.
Shit-plugged toilets.
Overflowing sharps containers
busted by addicts scrounging for dregs
of old blood with heroin
in used syringes.

Battalions of mental health workers
and cops swarm in
to this open door asylum.

## Enemy in the Mirror

There's a small towel
on my mirror. I'm hiding
from myself again,
but peek at the enemy
anyway.

Red face,
long, unwashed 4:30 AM hair,
wide, watery blue eyes
with red alligators swimming in them.

Seeing

a thief
a cheat
an outlaw
a hater of self
a working-class loser
or
an unknown hero.

But should shave anyway
before work.

# Welfare Wednesdays Kill More People than Bombs

*Dedicated to the Sedin Brothers, from a Boston Bruins Fan*

Hastings is closed off from Main Street
all the way down to Pigeon Park.
Cops, fire trucks, floodlights
making night into day.
The crowds grow, hoping
for a show. People set up
lawn chairs in the middle
of Hastings like they're at a drive-in.
Skateboarders fly down the emptiness
like dragonflies skimming a pond,
zigzagging around everything.
It's like a street party
or the gathering for a town hanging.

A twenty-year-old jumper in debt to his dealer
has climbed over the railing
on the roof across the street.
I sit at my window
drinking a beer, thinking
about wild horses running in the rain.

Cops roam around, telling the shouters to shut up.
The copper on the bullhorn bellows,
"Please stop telling the poor man to jump."

Finally, they talk the young dude down.
We all cheer as if the Canucks
have just scored the game-winning goal.

## Harm Reduction

It's 6 AM when the lights turn on
in a whitewashed drugstore.
It looks like a little theatre
shining out onto the sidewalk.

The regulars are there
walking around in tight circles
like chickens on hot plates
waiting for their next government fix.

Just before work, I always get hit up
for a smoke by Freddy Fridays.
He's from Toronto like me,
but a few years older,
remembering T.O. at its best
when it comes to sex, drugs and rock 'n' roll.

He's 6'1 and looks like a tobacco farmer from Tillsonburg
with his John Deere ball cap,
worn-out jeans and Levi's jacket.
A gaunt face of skin-wrapped bone,
long black hair, coal eyes,
teeth rotten and stained
with twenty years on the crack pipe,
arms full of the needle and the damage done,
a voice like smoky wind
spitting out dust about
the good ol' days of Toronto.

I give him a smoke. His nerves
light it right away as he stares
at that little lit stage, waiting

for his Methadone juice
and the next act.

I light myself a smoke and watch
the store next door unload
a dolly full of boxes labelled
with big blue letters spelling
LISTERINE.

## Sunday Morning Sidewalk

*For Ralph*

It's God's day off and mine too.
There are tents on every block and back alley now.
As I walk down sidewalks cleared by rain
to get a coffee and newspaper,
I complain to myself about the price of the paper.
But I need that crossword.
Wonder if this time I will finish it, although I never do.
In front of the Ovaltine restaurant, a five and a half foot woman
in a drenched grey hoodie weaves and flails
through Hastings Street traffic
like a scarecrow in the wind.
Horns blare at her "I don't give a shit" smile.

# The Room, Oppenheimer Park Lodge

Another concrete 8 by 10 foot room.
The suicide window opens only 6 inches
out onto a back alley.

I fight off hundreds of cockroaches
on the kitchen counter.

Beside the unmade single bed,
a writing desk with a lamp
and my old manual typewriter.
Heaps of papers.

Dead end poems
crumpled inside
a green steel garbage can.

My therapist is a bartender
at the Empress tavern.
She pours me a pint,
asks how I'm doing.

"I feel like Han Solo in carbonite,"
I reply. His poster's on my wall,
that frozen grimace,
hands locked in surrender.

# Washroom Journals

## i. Prep

The trees are blackened by hundreds of crows
as I walk to work for my 6 AM to 3 PM shift
at the Main and Hastings public washrooms,
built in 1923, open 6 AM to 12 AM,
seven days a week, every day of the year.
I open up the top gate, walk down 18 steps
to open the second gate.
With a flashlight, I find the keyhole to open
the main door, then the door to my office,
turn on all the lights, inside and out.
Put on gloves and a mask,
then bleach down the office, door knobs,
light switches, radio, table, fridge, chair,
dustpan, broom handle. Turn on CBC radio.
Next, go to the janitor's closet, fill the mop bucket
and toilet bucket with water and bleach.
Wipe down the whole washroom.
(No one cleans as good as I do.)
Finally, mop the floor, put up the signs:
"Caution: Wet Floors."

Only two stalls allowed to be occupied at a time.
After each use, I bleach the toilet, handle, stall walls,
latches, sinks, taps, faucets, paper towel dispenser.
Not much time to sit.

Standing at the steel gate behind a plexiglass shield,
I'm like a doorman, wearing a mask, bandanna
and rubber gloves, now ready
to let my first customers in.

## ii. Eighteen Steps

The taxi drivers in the coffee shop arrive first. A tall, well-dressed Asian dude with greased-back midnight hair comes down, Levi jeans tucked into cowboy boots, and a black belt in English. He never smiles, just says "Thanks, man. Have a good day."

The South Asians arrive next, talking about their 12-hour shifts, their half-English, half-Punjabi words sing through the underground washroom. Standing guard at the gate, I open it and greet them with "Good morning."

Then drug dealers, drug users, bus drivers, street people, construction workers, sanitation workers line up on the stairs, waiting to come in.

Throughout the day, a few Chinese seniors step gracefully down the steps, including one man with a big smile who sometimes gives me smokes. Watching out for them to make sure they're safe, I welcome them into this sanctuary.

### iii. The Phone Thief

Years ago, I signed into work at the SRO
while other staff were watching the news:
footage of a man in his twenties on the SkyTrain
who ripped off a cell phone from a woman in a wheelchair,
then ran out the door.
Everyone in the office recognized him —
a third-floor resident with a robot face,
eyes with nothing behind them.
We called the cops.

They showed up and we all went to his room.
The manager said, "You need a search warrant."
I looked at her. "I can check the room for safety issues."
The head detective in his suit and mustard-stained tie
smiled. Everyone smiled, even
my firecracker manager with her crossed arms.

I opened the door into his life:
a 6 by 8 foot room, fist-sized gouges in the drywall,
mattress covered with burns,
toaster with burned cigarette fossils on top.
"WTF" spray-painted in black on the far wall.
Syringes everywhere. I put on gloves, did my search.
No phone.

The cops arrested him by the end of the day.
On the evening news, that same detective grinned.
"We'd also like to thank a certain street detective
for helping us with this case."

Ten years later, the phone thief
comes down to the washroom where I work.
A few times a day, he shoots up, then comes by
the washroom attendants' office to put his syringes
into the needle exchange box, always
saying thank you. Never giving me any problem.

Some fall farther into life on the streets than others.
Some like me ran into it.
He was born into it.

## iv. Volcano Boy

One of the regulars comes down the steps
holding a skateboard and a handful of syringes.
He's skinny, like a stalk of celery with arms,
reminding me of myself at that age.
He heads for the last stall.
After fifteen minutes I walk down.
"Everything okay in there, kid?"
He looks up at me, his moon face pocked with pimples.
"Do you have any Band-Aids, Boss?" he asks politely.
He's sitting there on the toilet seat, digging
into scabby holes in his left forearm.
They look like a small forest of volcanoes
with rivers of blood.
"Holy shit! I will be right back."
I run to the office, put on fresh gloves, grab the first aid kit,
run back. I open a handful of alcohol prep-pads
so he can clean up his arm. Then,
gently, one at a time, I put a Band-Aid
over each little volcano.

## v. No Shelter

One morning at work, I hear an old man crying.
As I walk over to the last stall,
the smell of shit grows stronger.
"Everything okay in there, buddy?" I ask.
The stall door is partly open.
The man inside has wavy gray hair
and wears an oversized tweed jacket.
Ashamed and confused at the same time,
he's naked from the waist down.
His bright green eyes stare
at his soiled pants on the floor,
his hands spread apart in surrender.

"I had to sleep on the streets last night.
No room at the shelter.
I had a bad accident in my pants,"
he says in an elegant, intelligent voice.

"What do you need? I'm the janitor here."
Size 32 pants, underwear, socks.
But first he has to clean himself up.
I run to the paper towel dispenser, wet a stack,
return to the stall. "Here, take this.
Don't worry about the mess."

Then I run up to the First United
to get him underwear and pants,
but they don't have any socks.
To give the man time, I stop
at the bar for a quick beer.
Four swigs later, I'm off,
back to the washrooms.
He's still in the stall.

I give him the clothes,
peel off my winter work socks
and hand them to him.
I won't ever see him again,
but hope he's okay.

# The Pirate Artist

*For Alan Sayers*

You could always find him
at the Grand Union at Hastings and Abbott,
holding court every day with the regulars
at a table at the end of the bar.

A wiry beanstalk of a man
with short hair and nerdy glasses
like a character from *Mad Men*.

He'd lay out portraits:
Keith Richards, John Lennon,
Janis Joplin, Neil Young, Bob Dylan,
Bob Marley, even Trump
in pen and ink. His most popular picture: a crow
in oversized rubber rain boots,
smoking a joint.

For thirty years, like a hunter's powerful scope,
his sharp pen captured
the Carnegie, the Empress,
the Dominion Building, the Save On Laundry,
back alleys and more, while he played
Russian roulette with crack,
losing to a fentanyl bullet.

The day after his death,
the picture he gave me
falls off my wall.
He's saying goodbye
before leaving for good.

## Just Because We Live Here

I get on the bus after a ten-hour shift,
pay my $3 to just go a few blocks,
too tired to walk home.
I sit down in the first seat I see,
open the window and put on my mask.
A maskless man who wears a smile of hate
jumps up to close the window, then says loudly,
"Keep the window closed, you fuck'n junkie crackhead."
Just because we live here,
they think we're all the same.

But there's another side.
There's George who runs the barber shop beside the Empress Hotel
who always has a joke for us and sometimes cuts my hair for free.
Carlos, the community wise man selling hemp clothing at Serf to Surf,
who puts out a container of fresh water for the dogs.
My drinking buddies, regulars at the Empress, most of them retired:
Jimmy the Ferret, a longshoreman for twenty years;
Jimmy Mack, a stockbroker who got rich, then got poor three times in a row;
Brian, a part-time upholsterer;
Ralph, who worked for the railroad for thirty-three years;
David, a former building contractor who cleaned tour buses until last year;
Byron who lives upstairs at the Empress and worked in the sawmills;
Little Roy who worked in the sawmills too;
Hungarian Steve, a professional drywaller;
Benny who removed asbestos insulation at Woodwards.
The bartenders and waitresses at all the pubs —
The Empress, Pat's Pub, The Savoy, The West Hotel, Grand Union.
Ian who sells T-shirts he's designed.
Alan, the artist who sketched me in the bars and alleys.
Cartoon Mike who drew the best handmade birthday cards.
All the workers at the shelters.

Everyone at the Carnegie Centre,
like the red-headed lady security guard who's a kickboxer,
the DTES Writers Collective that meets every Thursday
run by Gilles, a retired carpenter who's twenty years sober,
Diane who sets out a big buffet of snacks,
putting tea lights on each table for monthly poetry readings.
All the street people who come to listen.
The guy and his girlfriend who come up to me, saying
"Thank you for writing about us."
Construction workers from the labour pools —
some young, some old, all tough.
Most of them too smart to be living here.
The Asian clerk at Garlane Pharmacy who sells me lottery tickets.
I tell her, "If I win, I'll buy you roses."
Young families bringing their kids to school.
A First Nations father who walks there with his three sons.
their long black hair in braids.
I smile at them, thinking
they are beautiful.

## A Drunk with a Typewriter

halfway through a case of beer
burning words into emptiness
through the banging of the keys

like a drowning man coming up for air
a starving man waiting for a free meal
a trapper eager for his next kill
like going through a storm
can't stop now

## Soul on Fire

I write because my soul is on fire.
All my sins and fears are here.
It's just another sick Tuesday
in the middle of the end
when time stops,
then cracks into two.
You'll find me there.

# Through All This

Born through all this
A three-storey house full of rats
Lived through all this
Dirty foster home to dirty foster home
Ran alone through all this
Slept under bridges through all this
Kept warm with pain and hate
Loved through all this
A flower that I didn't know how to water
Drank through all this
Skid row, skid row, skid row
Worked slave labour to survive through all this
Lost myself through all this
Found myself through all this
Typed down my madness through all this
Through all this
Felt real

## NOTES TO THE POEMS

"Remembrance Day": Three-time lightweight Canadian champion, Gaétan Hart, attended this fight along with his trainer and manager, all seated in the front row. They were scouting me for their boxing club.

"Death isn't lonely": I found out the next day that the dead homeless man had once been a well-known country music performer who'd made recordings.

"Drunken Laundry Day with Charles Bukowski" was turned into an award-winning animated video poem that has been selected for screening at DOXA documentary film festival, The Zebra International Poetry Film Festival in Germany, the Film & Video Poetry Symposium in Los Angeles and at several other local and international festivals. See https://vimeo.com/387885734.

"The DTES Alarm Clock": Former police constable, Dave Dickson is the White Knight of the DTES who worked the DTES beat from 1980-2008. He was the first officer who brought a list of missing women to the attention of Vancouver police. https://www.cbc.ca/news/canada/british-columbia/vicki-black-cold-case-dave-dickson-1.5383348

"The Untouchables": Ashley Machiskinic, 22, died after a five-storey fall from a Regent Hotel window in 2010. The word on the street was that she owed $50 to the men who pushed her out the window. Her murderers were never caught.
https://www.cbc.ca/news/indigenous/ashley-machiskinic-vancouver-death-1.3653676

"The Pirate Artist": The Grand Union is known among regulars as "The Grand Onion." Alan Sayers was a long-time friend, supporter, and artist who illustrated one of my chapbooks, but passed away recently. https://thetyee.ca/News/2021/04/08/Artist-Used-Crack-30-Years-Last-Hit-Contaminated/

"Just Because We Live Here": Cartoon Mike drew terrific personalized cards for friends. He used to do windows for a car dealership after working there as a salesman. Everyone saved his cards. He died too soon.

"Washroom Journals: Volcano Boy": The washroom stall doors are cut short so attendants can look into the stalls in case someone is overdosing or in other trouble.

"Soul on Fire" (formerly titled "Fuck the Poets"): A short musical version of this piece was performed in 2015 as part of *Voice to Voice*, a collaboration by Thursdays Writing Collective organized by Elee Kraljii Gardiner with students from UBC Music Faculty. Composer Lucas Oickle, internationally acclaimed tenor, Spencer Britten, and pianist Yekaterina Utegenova collaborated to put the poem to music under the title, "I write because my soul is on fire" :https://www.youtube.com/watch?v=Cva9Iefoz-w

## ACKNOWLEDGEMENTS

Thank you to the publications which published the original versions of my poems:

"All-Day Breakfast" in *From the Heart of It All: Ten Years of Writing from Vancouver's Downtown Eastside*, ed. Heidi Greco, Otter Press, 2018. "Broken Key" and "Death Isn't Lonely" in *V6A Writing from Vancouver's Downtown Eastside* (Arsenal Pulp Press, 2012). "Downtown Eastside Alarm Clock" in *Megaphone* #67, 2010 and *Poetry is Dead*, Issue 02, Volume 02. "Drunken Laundry Day with Charles Bukowski" in *Geist* #82 and *V6A: Writing from Vancouver's Downtown Eastside* (Arsenal Pulp Press, 2012). It also won the Downtown Eastside Writers Jamboree Contest in 2011. "Fuck the Poets" (now entitled "Soul on Fire") in *Voice to Voice* (Otter Press: 2015). "Ghost in the Closet" in *Voices of the Street*, Megaphone, 2017. "Harm Reduction" in *Geist*, #104, Spring, 2017. "Hey Joe" in *The Writers Caravan Anthology* (Otter Press, 2011). "Killing Me the Rest of the Way" in *Geist*, #104, Spring, 2020. "Pain and Wastings" in *Megaphone* #67, 2010. "Poetry of a Square Room" in *The Stanza Project* (Otter Press, 2013). "Refugees from Nowhere" *Megaphone* magazine, January 2016. "Rooming House Blues" in *Voices of the City* (*Megaphone*, 2010) and in *24 Hours*. "Shotguns in the Sky" in *Geist*, #104, Spring, 2017. "Sunday Morning Sidewalk" in *Geist*, #119, Summer 2021. "Underground Room" in *Thursdays 2: Writings from the Carnegie Centre*, eds. Elee Kraljii Gardiner and John Asfour, Otter Press, 2009, and *Geist*, #104, Spring, 2017. "The Untouchables," in *Megaphone*, Issue 67, November 26, 2010 and reprinted in the *Carnegie Newsletter*, January 15, 2011. "Welfare Wednesdays Kill More People than Bombs," in *Geist*, #104, Spring, 2017.

•. •. •

I also want to thank the following people and organizations:

Anvil Press and Publisher Brian Kaufman and staff. Amber Dawn who is an important part of the DTES arts community and who headed TWC one year. The Carnegie Centre. Eric Hall and Esmeralda Cabral for formatting my past chapbooks. Charles "Carlos" Herbst for his artwork and ongoing support of my poetry. Steven Hill, a good man who was a DTES social worker that befriended me through poetry. Patrick Holloway and Annabel Buckley, my former teachers in Ottawa. AnnMarie MacKinnon and *Geist* magazine for having faith in my work. Isabella Mori and the judges of the Muriel's Journey contest. *Megaphone* magazine for supporting DTES writers and vendors and publishing my work. Alan Sayers, my artist friend. May he rest in peace. Kevin Spenst for making me walk out on that pirate plank and making me jump. Richard Tetrault for his artwork for the cover and interior of the book. Diane Wood, coordinator of the Carnegie Centre Poetry Reading series. Everyone at Thursdays Writing Collective (TWC), now called the Downtown Eastside Writers Collective, coordinated by Gilles Cyrenne. The Vancouver Foundation in partnership with the Carnegie Community Centre that runs the DTES Small Arts Grants Program that funded my two chapbooks and my poetry video. The Woodcock Fund and James Davies of The Writers Trust of Canada for financial assistance. Marc Perez, a fellow poet and tenant support worker at Lookout. Word Vancouver and Executive Director Bonnie Nish for including me in the festival. Daniel Zomparelli, former editor of *Poetry is Dead*.

Huge thanks to my coach, mentor, guide, scribe, muse, Vulcan mind-melder and editor, Fiona Tinwei Lam, who started working with me through the DTES Manuscript Intensive organized by The Writers' Studio and the Carnegie Centre back in 2012, after having been on the jury that awarded me *Geist* magazine's 2011 DTES Writers' Jamboree prize. Thank you for championing and publicizing my work, assisting me with getting grants and interviews, probing me with questions to deepen my poems, submitting my work to magazines and contests, producing my video poem, and inspiring me to write more about my childhood, my junkyard job, and my janitorial work. Through our regular meetings and phone calls over many years, you helped turn my journal entries, stories, and notes into poems, and typed, revised, collated, and assembled this poetry manuscript when my old laptop kept breaking down.

I am also extremely thankful to Elee Kraljii Gardiner, Coordinator of Thursdays Writing Collective (TWC) 2009-2018 for her inspiration, encouragement, kindness, generosity and continuing support. You published and publicized the work of DTES poets like myself over many years in amazing ways. You have both been lighthouses in a storm.

## ABOUT THE AUTHOR

Henry Doyle lives and works in Vancouver's Downtown Eastside. A long-time member of Thursdays Writing Collective and the Downtown Eastside Writing Collective, Henry has published work in *Poetry is Dead*, *Megaphone*, *Geist*, the anthologies *V6A: Writing from Vancouver's Downtown Eastside* and *From the Heart of it All: Ten Years of Writing from Vancouver's Downtown Eastside*. He won *Geist* magazine's DTES Jamboree Writing Contest in 2011 and Muriel's Journey Poetry Prize in 2020.

PHOTO: MARINA DODIS